# The Vale of Kashmir

John Isaac

# The Vale of Kashmir

Introduction by Art Davidson

W. W. Norton & Company | New York  London

*For the people of Kashmir,*

*my late mother, Thangam,*

*and my wife, Jeannette.*

JACKET: The Hazratbal Mosque in Srinagar is the most revered shrine of the Kashmiris. Its history dates to the early seventeenth century.

PAGES 2–3: Houseboat on Dal Lake after a storm.

LEFT: Betab Valley. Glacial waters of Lidder River. People come from all over to fish in the river, which is famous for its trout.

PAGES 6–7: Panoramic view of Dal Lake taken from a hill known as Takht-I-Sulaiman in the southeast of Srinagar.

# Contents

View of Dal Lake from Takht-I-Sulaiman showing the famous
floating gardens of Kashmir (the green strips), which have been in
existence for more than five hundred years. The floating base is made
from the bulrush plant and usually measures about 300 feet long by
10 feet wide. Then this is filled up with seaweed and other vegetation
taken from the lake bottom. Melons, cucumbers, and tomatoes all
grow amazingly well on these tiny islands in the lake.

View of Nehru Park area of Dal Lake.

# Preface

*If there is paradise on earth, it is here, it is here, it is here.*
— THE MOGHUL EMPEROR JAHANGIR, DESCRIBING
KASHMIR AND HIS BELOVED MOGHUL GARDENS

Growing up in a small village in tropical southern India, I used to wonder what snow was like in faraway Kashmir. I also dreamed of having a glass of the famous Gold Coin apple juice made with apples from Kashmir, but it was too expensive for my family and I never had the chance to try it.

More often, though, Kashmir came to my attention through family discussions about the land as a source of dispute between Pakistan and India. Ever since partition in 1947, when the British left India and Pakistan was created as a Muslim country, Kashmir has been claimed by both sides. In 1965, when war broke out for the second time between Pakistan and India over Kashmir and the dispute again grabbed world headlines, I was twenty-two years old and living with my mother in the metropolis of Madras, now called Chennai, where we had moved in 1959.

The big city whet my appetite to see more of the world, and so in 1968, I left India with my twelve-string guitar, hoping to become a folksinger. When I landed in New York City I had only 75 cents in my pocket and no place to stay. I contacted a friend, who very generously invited me to stay in his apartment. Eventually, I managed to get a job as a messenger at the United Nations when a woman I had met who belonged to the UN choral group thought I'd be a good addition and helped me apply for a job.

When an opening became available in the photography unit as a darkroom technician, I applied and got the post. It was then that I was given a book by the French photographer Henri Cartier-Bresson. I was immediately drawn to a photograph he had taken in 1948 in Kashmir showing women praying at dawn against the backdrop of the Himalayas. I made a vow to visit Kashmir as soon as possible.

However, many years would pass before I had the opportunity to make this long-awaited trip. I had been promoted to photographer at the United Nations and in that capacity had traveled to more than a hundred countries, including Afghanistan and Pakistan, but I had never been sent to Kashmir, where UN troops have been stationed since shortly after partition. Finally, in October 2003, when I was in Delhi and hunting around for a good story, a friend suggested I do something on Kashmir, where she was involved in the Kashmiri handicraft business. I was on a plane within a few days.

When I landed in Srinagar, the capital of Jammu and Kashmir, as the country is officially called, it was a cool, crisp October day. I descended into the cacophony produced by travelers, honking bus and taxi horns, and merchants selling their wares. Watching all were Indian army troops standing at the periphery of the airport. I was in the Indian portion of Kashmir. In 1972 a Line of Control dividing the region in two was established, but it has not diminished the tension that still exists between the two nuclear powers. The Pakistanis call their side Azad Kashmir.

As I traveled out of the city heading for a houseboat on Dal Lake, I began to relax and enjoy my surroundings. Soon I was resting comfortably in one of the famous Clermont houseboats where royalty and rock stars such as George Harrison once stayed. A kind man named Abdul served me kava tea made with almonds, cardamom seeds, and cinnamon, a Kashmiri specialty. As I surveyed the majestic mountains surrounding the lake, I was already captivated and knew I had made the right decision to come here.

Fishing village near Hazratbal area on Dal Lake.
The government will soon dismantle these illegal cottages.

Early the next morning I took a ride in a *shikara*, the Kashmiri version of a gondola. I had no way of knowing that Lassa, the shikara driver, would become my guide and friend over my next nine trips to Kashmir.

As we wandered leisurely around the lake, I saw many houseboats where multiple families lived, as well as a thriving community selling and trading vegetables from the floating gardens that had made Dal Lake famous. Later, I learned that the lake is terribly polluted and that plant debris and garbage thrown into the lake was making it shallow, threatening its very survival.

Just a few weeks after that first trip, Lassa called me in New York to tell me that the saffron harvest was about to begin. Saffron is an important crop in Kashmir, and so I hurried back to get there in time. We traveled to the village of Pampore, 16 kilometers north of Srinagar, where I saw hundreds of people working in fields, painstakingly gathering up crocus flowers. I noticed that around the fringes of the fields men were trying to barter cheap Chinese-made flashlights and batteries for crocus flowers. They knew the flowers would bring them a lot of money, but there were no takers. The Kashmiris needed every single crocus flower they could pick, since it takes thousands of them to make just one ounce of saffron.

Kashmir is not well known to the outside world as a producer of saffron, but it is world renowned for its abundance of superb handicrafts: carpets, shawls, silks, woodwork, and papier-mâché boxes. Throughout the region's history, trade routes and their offshoots between China and the West wove their way through the mountain passes of Kashmir, bringing in desirable items such as silver, salt, tea, and spices while major exports have included saffron, shawls, and silks.

Srinagar is where the finest pashmina shawls are woven. A friend of mine who has a showroom of Kashmiri products in Delhi sent me to see a family of weavers in their home after I had visited Pampore. The man who

Family going to the marketplace on their *shikara* (typical Kashmiri boat) in Hazratbal on Friday to sell *hak*, a favorite vegetable of the Kashmiris. While there, they will also visit the mosque for Friday prayers.

was doing the embroidery claimed the paisley design came from Kashmir, but the teardrop shape most likely originated in Persia in the sixteenth century. The embroiderer told me it could take from six months to a year to complete a finely detailed shawl.

In the summer of 2004 I returned to Kashmir to observe the Hindu pilgrimage to the Amarnath caves above Lake Sheshnag in the east. Pilgrims come by the thousands to worship a stalagmite ice formation representing a phallic form of the creator Shiva.

After an arduous four-hour car ride from Srinagar, Lassa and I spent the night in Pahalgam, where a lot of pilgrims had already gathered for the final ascent to Sheshnag. We rose early the next morning to travel by foot up the steep 27-kilometer trail leading to Sheshnag. By the time we arrived it was evening and freezing cold. I was not at all prepared for the 12,000-foot altitude, and without a jacket or sleeping bag, I nearly froze to death that night. As we huddled in the tent that had been set up, I proposed bringing in some of the mules and horses to help us keep warm, but no one else liked my idea.

After a fitful night's sleep, I woke before dawn and watched the sun rise over the spectacular snowcapped mountains. That alone made the hard trek and the cold night worthwhile. Lake Sheshnag was very still and pristine, with an occasional bird flying overhead. Hundreds of Hindus were stirring in their tents, getting ready to continue past the lake and up to the caves. I thought about the day before, when I was touched to see Kashmiri porters—Gujars—carrying the Hindu pilgrims up the steep path, willingly repeating the Hindu slogan, over and over again, *Har, Har, Mahadev* (Hail Lord Shiva). The Gujars are cattle-rearing Muslims who make extra money by providing mules and horses for this annual pilgrimage as well as serving as porters.

After drinking tea, Lassa and I were happy to head back down the mountain, taking twice as long as usual because I stopped so many times to take photographs.

One of the canals connected to Dal Lake. The water comes from natural springs and melting snow from the mountains.

16

Among my favorite villages in Kashmir is Rezan, one of the towns and villages we passed through as we drove up to Sonamarg in the northeast. Sonamarg is in the beautiful Sindh Valley and, at an altitude of some 9,000 feet, has breathtaking scenes of snowcapped glaciers. I passed through Rezan many times and always stopped to photograph simple village scenes featuring buildings with pastel-colored walls. Rezan is inhabited primarily by Gujars, many of whom have settled down to become shepherds and farmers.

Mamar is another town on the Srinagar-Sonamarg route, and one time when I was there on a Friday in the bitter cold of winter I stopped at the Usmaniya Jamia mosque. I received permission from the mullah to photograph inside the mosque during the Friday prayers. Despite the frigid weather, about one hundred men and women were squeezed into the small space. At some point, two young men came over and pushed me and said, "Religion, no photos." I stopped and tried to explain that I had the mullah's permission, but of course they didn't understand me. Finally the mullah ordered them to leave me alone and I was able to continue. Afterward, outside the mosque, I showed the photographs to the two men and asked them—through Lassa, who translated—if they saw anything objectionable. Once they saw the pictures they realized there was no bad intention on my part and everything was okay.

This was a rare confrontation for me. Indeed, I found the Kashmiris I met on my trips very kind and hospitable. Often, they asked me to have tea or dinner with them. When they found out I was working on a book, they urged me not to cover the problems between India and Pakistan but instead to concentrate on the beauty of their country.

Another part of the beauty of Kashmir is its people. My guide Lassa never went to school and doesn't know how to read or write. But his knowledge of life and nature is vast, beyond that of anyone else I have ever met. Several times he invited me to his home, where I met his mother, his wife, and their four children, including a little boy he adopted who had been abandoned. He is also caring for his sister, who was abandoned by her husband. He is a true Sufi, tolerant and caring for others. I'd like to think that I absorbed some of his Sufi values as I traveled with him throughout Kashmir.

One of Lassa's favorite expressions is *inshallah*, meaning God willing. Lassa said it constantly and explained that it means we humans are not in control of everything, that we have to leave some things to a higher being. My dream for Kashmir—and the purpose of this book—is to show what a beautiful country this is and for people from all over the world to come and enjoy Kashmir and its people. *Inshallah.*

John Isaac

Between the villages of Anantnag and
Avantipura boys take their horses home.

# In The Vale of Kashmir

ART DAVIDSON

In the stillness before dawn a plaintive call to morning prayer echoes across Dal Lake. It is early spring in Srinagar, and as the darkness softens, mosques fill with men dressed in full-length *farins* who come for their first prayers of the day.

With the first light seeping through the mist, flocks of myna birds that slept all night in banyan trees fly off to villages and fields in search of insects, grubs, seeds, and scraps. Roosters crow, their flocks of hens and chicks scattering to scavenge along the roadside. Men rowing their narrow *shikaras* move quietly across the lake; their wives, bundled up against the morning chill, bring to market eggs, vegetables, fruits, and things their hands have made. A heron alights in tall grass and begins its silent vigil for an unwary minnow.

The pulse of the city quickens with the honking of drivers hurrying through the narrow streets and merchants hawking bread, fruit, rugs, cups, shirts. Kites soar and dip on agile wings over a path where they know someone will sooner or later throw out some morsel they can eat. Far above the domed mosques and patchwork of rooftops and chimneys sending up thin curls of smoke, the mist clears. The sun strikes a high, snow-lined peak.

As sunlight touches one knoll after another and begins flooding through trees, I feel I could be watching the sunrise from my home in Alaska. I have come to Kashmir from the far side of the world. Yet as I travel

Bridge across the Sindh River to Rezan village.

about the country and catch a glimpse of glaciers in the distance and the gray-green tint of glacial silt in the mountain streams, a trout leaping from a pool to catch a fly, meadows of wildflowers, an eagle soaring through the clouds . . . well, there are moments when the resemblance to Alaska is so keen that I feel I have been here before. Though in truth Kashmir is like no other place on earth.

The Vale of Kashmir is the green heart of this region where India, China, and Pakistan meet. The wide valley runs through Jammu and Kashmir for about 135 kilometers. Surrounded by towering peaks of the Pir Panjal and the Himalayas, the Vale is a vast garden dotted with lakes, marshes, orchards, and terraced fields. The ancient city of Srinagar spreads along the shores of five interlocking lakes, including Dal Lake with its floating gardens and many canals lined with houseboats. Throughout the Vale there are sounds of running water—rivulets, streams, and waterfalls coming off the peaks, joining and rejoining as they form rivers that eventually flow into the Jhelum, which meanders through the Vale before plunging down to the plains of Punjab.

In summer, Himalayan black bears are out of their dens and wandering about. The blue mountain sheep of Kashmir and Ladakh graze up to 16,000 feet. In the high meadows shepherds keep a watchful eye for eagles that can swoop down and carry away a lamb. The woods and glens resonate with the songs of Kashmiri birds—thrushes, finches, golden orioles, and cuckoos— more than three hundred species in all. In winter, snow leopards that spent the summer months among rocky cliffs at tree line follow both sheep and the elusive hangul deer to lower elevations. The marshes spill over with millions of migrating waterfowl flying in from Siberia and Mongolia.

At an elevation of about 5,500 feet, the Vale is blessed with a temperate climate. From Kashmir's first king in 2,500 BC, one dynasty after another has been drawn to the Vale to escape the heat of the Indian plains. In the seventeenth century, Moghul emperors built an imposing summer palace that still stands above Srinagar; beyond the city lie gardens they laid out in Nishat and Shalimar. In spring the air carries the scent of

Near Mamar women go to the mountains in the early morning to cut wood for fuel.

roses and of blossoms that by autumn will become apples, pears, peaches, and plums.

Traveling through Kashmir feels like a journey to another time. I feel this walking through the open markets and winding alleyways of Srinagar and in the countryside. Two old men riding donkeys pause on the road to talk. Boys play with sticks along a riverbank. A man and his wife shovel straw and dung into baskets they carry to fields they'll soon plant. A shepherd climbs a ladder to reach dried branches he cut and stashed in a tree. He is old, but his arms and legs move gracefully as he balances on the top rung of the ladder and reaches for some leafy branches to feed to his sheep waiting below.

To reach the little village of Rezan on the way to Sonamarg and Ladakh I must cross a wooden bridge that spans a raging torrent. I'm sitting in someone's home drinking tea when the father of the family motions for me to follow him up the stairs. At the top, we climb a ladder to an open loft where sickles and rakes, bags of summer clothes, and stacks of hay are stored. To one side, his parents and several others are kneeling before a loom, carefully guiding threads of wool with their fingertips. They use small hooks to tighten each loop in place. It will take them six months or more to make just one traditional Kashmiri rug. It is the same with every artisan I meet: whether weaving a rug, etching a silver vase, embroidering a shawl, or painting a papier-mâché doll or jewelry box, they take whatever time they need to make each stitch or touch just right.

This unhurried pace, so different from the rhythms of life in the West, is etched in the footpaths that connect one hillside village to another and in the way small mosques are spaced just close enough so neighbors have time to walk to their place of prayer five times a day.

Today, most Kashmiris are Muslim. However, it has been a gradual transition to Islam and this has allowed Kashmiris time to integrate nuances of faith from people moving across Asia. From the earliest of times, caravans laden with linens, spices, and handicrafts journeyed from the plains of India to trade with caravans from China and Tibet bearing tea, silk, and wool. With the merchants came wandering scholars, monks, and

People visiting the famous Shalimar Gardens, built by the Moghul emperor Jahangir in the seventeenth century for his wife.

mendicants. Kashmir became a meeting ground for Buddhists bound for Tibet and Mongolia, Taoists from China, Hindus from India, and Muslims from Afghanistan and Pakistan. There were periods when Kashmiris came in contact with the civilizations of Rome, Greece, and Persia.

As this great flux of people passed through the Vale of Kashmir, their beliefs and spiritual yearnings intermingled in an atmosphere of tolerance. Hindu Brahmanism replaced earlier forms of Naga worship with barely a hint of persecution. When Buddhism came into ascendancy in the second century AD, thousands of monks sometimes gathered on the shores of Dal Lake; they dedicated new temples to Hindu as well as Buddhist deities. Many times Kashmir served as a refuge from religious persecution in other parts of Asia. Bamzai, a Pandit-Kashmiri scholar who has written extensively on the history of Kashmir, notes that even during the darkest periods of religious persecution and fanaticism elsewhere in Asia "the people of Kashmir lived amicably, giving what little solace, shelter, and comfort they could to their brothers in distress."

As Muslim merchants began coming in the twelfth and thirteen centuries to Kashmir to trade, there were scattered conversions to Islam. However, the defining moment came in 1320. King Rinchin, a Buddhist married to a Hindu, was undecided about which religion to adopt. In a dream, a voice told him to follow the faith of the first person he met the following day. The next morning he went out into the street and met Bulbul Shah, a Muslim Sufi saint from Turkistan. Taken with the Sufi's piety and gentle, egalitarian wisdom, Rinchin converted and made Islam the official faith of Kashmir. The people of the Vale began developing their own indigenous strain of Sufism, known as the Rishi order, within the fold of Islam.

I ask Lassa, a gracious sixty-year-old man who is helping me as a translator, what being a Sufi means to him.

"Sufis want to have everyone happy," he says smiling. After pausing for a moment, he continues, "Some people believe only what's written in the Holy Koran. They are not the Sufi. We follow the teachings of our beloved prophet, but we are also open to new ideas."

Two men in a window of the shrine in Ashmukam.

Children watch the road that leads to Sonamarg in the northeast.

Lassa takes me to the shrine of Sheikh Noor-ud-Din, the most revered saint of the Rishis, who affectionately call him Nund Rishi. As a child he had no formal education and spent much of his youth in quiet solitude. Over time he became a mystic and wrapped his thoughts in verses rich with simile and metaphor.

"Nund Rishi was a very good person for Kashmir and a great Muslim," says Lassa. "When he was walking he was making Sufi songs. In those days, we had a lot of Hindus, Sikhs, Christians, and Buddhists, as well as Muslims. He was treating everyone so nicely. With him, everyone was equal. No difference between people. He was very fine Sufi man. All over Kashmir, people honor him and try to be like him.

"For me, being a good Sufi Muslim is trying to live my life like Nund Rishi lived. I try to help others no matter what their faith. I try to treat everyone with kindness and love."

Rumi, the great Sufi poet, spoke of much the same. "There are no edges to my loving now," he wrote about the time when Islam was taking root in Kashmir in the thirteenth century:

> A church, a temple, or a kabala stone,
> Quran or Bible, or martyr's bone,
> All these and more my heart can tolerate
> Since my religion now is love alone.

"The Sufi's religion *is* love alone," says Mohammad Hassnain, coauthor of *The Sufi Alchemy of Peace*. "Love does not judge, love does not condemn, love tries to understand and respect the other's point of view."

For more than four centuries, Muslim Rishis have been reaffirming this Sufi vision of spiritual self-realization. Islamic scholars have come to recognize that Kashmir occupies a special place in the history of Islam, one that promotes traditions of tolerance, faith, friendliness, and care for others.

Ironically, the very fact that Kashmir is an Islamic culture, benevolent and tolerant as Sufis are, became a tipping point to conflict in 1947. British rule of the Indian subcontinent had come to an end. The partition that separated Pakistan from India left Kashmir caught between the two emerging powers. Kashmir's fate rested in the hands of its last maharaja, Hari Singh, who vacillated between joining Islamic Pakistan or India with its Hindu society.

Pakistan's new president, Mohammed Ali Jinnah, said that Kashmir could choose to be independent. However, many influential Pakistanis already thought of Kashmir and its Muslim people as part of their country. To enforce this sense of cultural imperative Pakistan invaded. Maharaja Singh, who might otherwise have sided with Pakistan, asked India for help. India answered with the stipulation, If you join us we will come to your rescue. Singh agreed and Kashmir's spiritual leader Sheikh Abdullah acquiesced on the condition that Kashmir would retain a large measure of self-rule. So it was that Jammu and Kashmir became a state within India yet caught in a prolonged tug-of-war between India and Pakistan.

Over the years, the conflict has taken more resources and lives than either India or Pakistan can afford. Periods of relative peace have been punctuated by gun battles, sometimes at 20,000 feet on the Siachen Glacier, and threats of nuclear retaliation. In 1954 India began incrementally to usurp Kashmir's self-rule. By 1972 a 742-kilometer Line of Control became a de facto boundary. It recognized Pakistan's control over the portion of Kashmir that is now called Azad Kashmir and ceded a smaller area to China. The Line of Control stretches over isolated mountains, but in places it runs through the middle of villages, separating families who must call to each other across barriers of concertina wire. The line helped maintain an uneasy truce, but much like the Berlin Wall had done, it divides a people who yearn to be united and free.

Throughout Kashmir one hears the call for *azadi*—freedom. To be free in their own country. Free to elect their own officials. Free to determine their own future. Free to raise their children with a sense of hope and purpose.

In the long run, restoring Kashmir's self-rule benefits the people of India as well. India once guaranteed Kashmir self-rule in all matters except defense, foreign affairs, currency, and communications. To be true to its own great heritage, India needs to be true to its word and to the Kashmiri people. This isn't just morally right, it's the only way India can build a lasting peace and let its people enjoy the inherent goodwill of their Kashmiri neighbors.

Alone on an empty road or finding my way among sheds and houses in a village, I felt safer in Kashmir than I would walking the streets of many American cities. Time and again, people motioned for me to come in, to sit with their family and drink tea. More often than not, the conversation turned to their children.

On the road to Ladakh, a Gujar man waves to me. His face is deeply tanned and lined, and as we talk he strokes his beard. His people are a minority within Kashmir. In summer they take their flocks of sheep and goats up into the mountains. Last fall he had to chase a bear out of his cherry tree. I tell him, with Lassa translating, that where I live I've had to do the same. He tells me that one night in his hut in the high meadows he was awakened by what he thought was an earthquake. He ran outside to find that the sound was a leopard fighting his dog on the roof. He hit the leopard with his coat and, as it ran away, the leopard slapped him in the face with its tail. We laugh. He's quiet.

"It's a good life up in the mountains," he says. "The streams are clear. Flowers everywhere. But my son tells me to sell our sheep. He doesn't want to herd sheep all his life. He wants to get an education. I can't read. But I'd like to make my son a good person. I'd like him to be a doctor or an engineer. Or other good educated person."

On the streets in Srinagar, people say the leaders of India and Pakistan could sit down and make peace in an afternoon. The Line of Control can be softened, Kashmir's self-rule restored.

There are, of course, many lines of control running throughout the world. Prejudice and intolerance. Barriers of culture and belief transect the lives of people everywhere. In America too.

Mohandas Gandhi once said that Kashmir represents our best chance to get it right. I want to hear Lassa say again how his religion is making others happy. I want to listen to Sufis like Mohammad Hassnain talk about how compassion, love, tolerance, sympathy, and happiness all come with the turning of the human heart.

Two boys fishing on Dal Lake,
with the village of Habak in the background.

# The Vale of Kashmir

Temple priest on the terrace of the Hanuman temple; the Jhelum
River, which runs through Srinagar, is in the background.

This photograph of a houseboat on the Jhelum River
was taken from Amira Kadal. (*Kadal* means bridge.)
This is a two-story houseboat that has at least six families
living in it. Today there are only a few boats like this in Srinagar.

In the spring seaweed is gathered to use as part of the base for the floating gardens. Bamboo poles are used to twist the weeds and pull them up from the lake bottom. Here the seaweed that was collected is being transported.

A floating garden is being moved to a new location for the summer.

OVERLEAF: Men gathering seaweed from the bottom of Dal Lake with a long bamboo pole. The seaweed is also used as fertilizer for the floating gardens.

OPPOSITE: A fisherman and his father as seen from my houseboat on Dal Lake. These fishermen live on the lake throughout the year.

ABOVE: A fisherman casts his net on Dal Lake. Fishing is the second largest industry of the region.

ABOVE: A fisherman and a kingfisher, both hoping for a good catch.

OPPOSITE: A kingfisher with its catch.

ABOVE: At the Hazratbal Friday market a *shikara* arrives with produce
to be sold.

OPPOSITE: Sunset on the lake, when everyone heads home and
everything becomes calm.

Around 4:30 a.m., the vendors meet to fix the prices of the produce
before heading to the floating market.

A man sells flowers on Dal Lake. People travel around the lake on their *shikaras* selling everything from fruit and drinks to woolen shawls, to leather goods, and other necessities of life to people in their houseboats.

In the starkness of winter, vendors transport onions and other produce through the small canals to various points in Srinagar.

Vendors with their produce start gathering at the floating market at
around 5 a.m. and usually stay until around 8 or 9 a.m.

Transporting bedspreads.

An open-air barbershop in the Hazratbal market area.

Roadside traders and vendors in the village of Kangan. The man in
the left foreground is sharpening knives and other tools.

Mother and child at Hazratbal market.

Lal Bazaar in Srinagar. Kashmir is famous for its apples.

Tea shop in the bus depot town of Kangan.

The main wholesale market in Srinagar, where fruits and produce
come from various parts of India.

A bakery in Srinagar. Kashmiris love their bread at all times of day, especially at breakfast.

ABOVE: Mother and daughter sell bread in Srinagar. There are more than fifteen different varieties of bread in Kashmir, including kulcha, sheermal, baqerkhani, and tsot.

OPPOSITE: In Pahalgam, a mother and daughter grind flour at a mill that is powered by a stream.

The main market in Srinagar.

A gift shop sells packages of dates, pistachios, almonds, and cashews
for festive occasions.

A family harvests saffron in the village of Pampore.

A girl gathers saffron flowers. It takes more than forty-five hundred crocus flowers to make one ounce of saffron.

The separation of the stigma from the flower is a tedious process
requiring a lot of patience.

This man is trimming the extended part of the stigma.

Kangan. A view of the Himalayas with fields of yellow mustard
flowers in the foreground.

In Kullen grass is cultivated and grown for cattle. In October the harvesting is done, as shown here.

ABOVE: Kullen. Women carry the bundles of harvested grass.

OPPOSITE: Farmer plowing a cornfield near the village of Mamar.

View of the valley from the road between Kullen and Rezan.

A grandfather and children wait for a bus near Sonamarg.

Women work in a rice field near Srinagar.

Apple picking in Pattan.

Women bring home branches from which they will make kangri baskets.
The baskets are then filled with coal and used in the winter to warm
people's hands.

ABOVE: Individual families grow silkworms and then sell the cocoons
to the government.

OPPOSITE: A field of mulberry plants near Pattan. The leaves are used
to feed silkworms.

A family thrashes rice on the outskirts of Srinagar.

A man and his flock of geese on the outskirts of Srinagar.

Srinagar. A grandmother spins pashmina wool while her grandchildren do homework. When the spinning is done, the yarn is sold back to the middleman who in turn will sell it to weavers to make shawls.

A clothing shop in Srinagar.

ABOVE: A carpet factory in Srinagar. The origin of the Kashmiri carpets is Persia.

OPPOSITE: Family of weavers who live on Dal Lake. The lake is shrinking so the government is trying to get families like this to move inland.

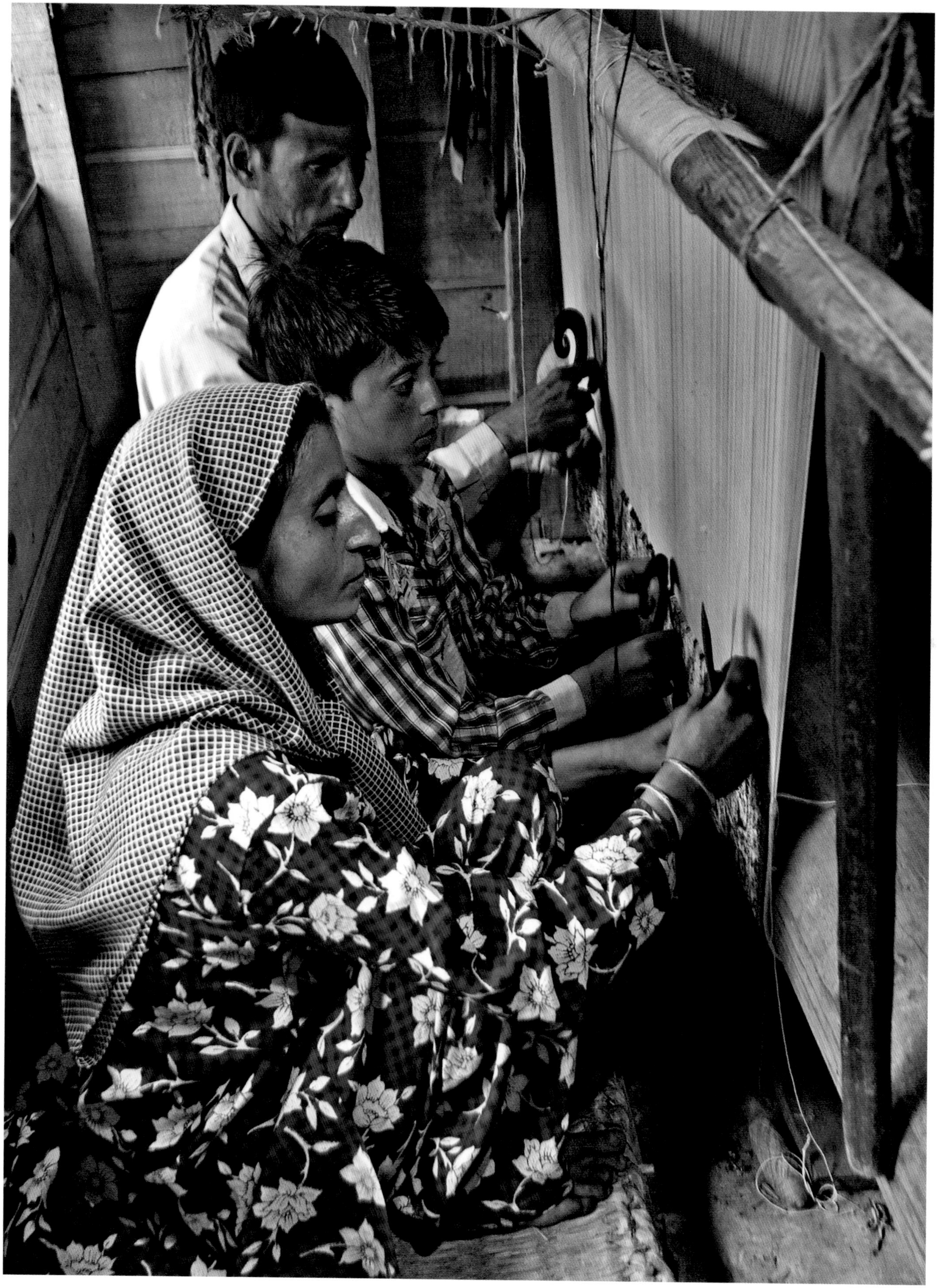

ABOVE: Carpet factory in Srinagar. The owner and workers are inspecting carpets.

OPPOSITE: A man embroiders a pashmina shawl. Other families did the spinning and weaving. It could take from six months to a whole year to complete a finely detailed shawl like this one.

Yarn shop in Srinagar.

Goldsmiths working in Srinagar.

On the way to Pattan, a man near the Hokersar wetlands works papier-mâché, one of the popular handicrafts of Kashmir.

ABOVE: Clay potters, in between Avantipura and Pampore.

OPPOSITE: Two men saw a poplar tree, in the traditional way, near Srinagar.

A father and son walk to their home near Kullen.

By the banks of the Sindh River, near Rezan.

At an old wooden bridge in Rezan, a father and son gather cow dung from which they make a paddy, dry it, and use it for fuel.

The village of Rezan in winter.

OPPOSITE: People walk toward Chandanwari.

The Gilgul Pass on the way to Sheshnag,
at an elevation of 12,000 feet.

ABOVE: Pilgrims walk up the pass heading toward Sheshnag on the way to
Amarnath Cave. The mules carry their food and water supply.

OPPOSITE: Pilgrims at Gilgul Pass on their yearly pilgrimage to Amarnath Cave.

Pilgrims and Hindu priests rest with Indian soldiers at
Pishu Top (10,400 feet) before reaching Sheshnag.

Gujars carry Hindu pilgrims who are not able to walk
to Amarnath Cave.

Hindu priests rest at the base camp in Chandanwari.

Shia women during the procession of Muharram in Srinagar.
The traditional Muharram procession marks the martyrdom of
Imam Hussain, the grandson of the Prophet Muhammad.

A shrine at Ashmukam.

ABOVE AND OPPOSITE: A Sunday gathering at a Sikh temple, or *gurdwara*, in Srinagar.

A mullah has a discussion with his congregation after Friday prayers
in Mamar.

The Patthar Masjid (Stone Mosque) in the old part of Srinagar. It is believed to have been built in 1623 by the empress Nur Jahan who, upon being questioned about the cost of its construction, pointed to her jeweled slippers and supposedly said, "As much as that." To this day, because of this legend, it is not a very popular place of worship.

Friday prayers at Jamia Mosque in Srinagar.

Friday prayers at a small mosque in Mamar.

Muharram procession in Srinagar.

A Koranic school in a Tibetan Muslim home in Srinagar. In the twelfth century a small band of Kashmiri traders traveled to Tibet and settled there. In the 1960s, following the Chinese invasion of Tibet, some of these Tibetan Muslims returned to Srinagar, where a little over one thousand are now living.

The entrance to the Shah Hamdan shrine. Built of wood in 1395,
this is one of the oldest mosques in Kashmir.

Distribution of bread to the poor at the Shah Hamdan shrine.

Women praying at Shah Hamdan.

A mother waters a plant at the martyrs' grave in Srinagar,
remembering her son, who was killed by the Indian army.

The Indian army is checking the identity of people who are traveling in Gund.

Rezan. A Gujar family in front of their house. The Gujars are Muslims who were once nomads and thought to have originated in Gujarat.

A family in front of their stone house in Sumbal.

Children posing in front of their home in Rezan.

Young woman in front of a Gujar house in Theni.

Shanty houses near Jhelum River.

A Gujar father and son in their modest home in Sonamarg.

Women chatting in
Ashmukam village.

A two-story house in Kullen.

A mother at home with her children in Rezan. Bamboo woven baskets called *kangri* with burning coal inside keep the hands warm in the winter.

A Gujar home in Nara Nag. The mother prepares dinner for the family
while her son sleeps on her lap and her father-in-law takes a nap.
Her sister, who is visiting from another village, will stay for dinner.

Mother and child in Rezan.

A father holding his newborn son in Atnar village near Pahalgam.

ABOVE: A young girl in front of her home in Mamar.

OPPOSITE: Mother and her newborn child in Atnar.

A woman prepares the midday meal at Pampur.

A woman prepares tea for her guests in Ganiwan. Every Kashmiri
home will have this teapot called a samovar.

Early in the morning villagers wash their
pots and pans in a canal adjoining Dal Lake.

Morning milk delivery in the downtown area of Srinagar.

142

Churning milk to
make a drink called
*lassi* (buttermilk).

Migrant workers (Shia community) from the Kargil area in the northeast
have come down to Kullen to grow grass, rice, corn, and walnuts.

A small middle school in Freslan near Pahalgam.

High school girls do their homework in Srinagar.

Children play cricket in the winter in Srinagar.

A young girl batting in Rezan.

Men play cricket in the winter on the way to Ghandarbal.

Children play high in the mountains of Gilgul Pass.

Schoolgirls on a picnic during holidays in Sonamarg.

A small mosque in Gund.

Bridge over the Lidder River near the village of Aru.

A Bakkarwal shepherd in the springtime in the Ganderbal district.
The Bakkarwals are nomadic people found in both Jammu and the
Kashmir Valley. They move along the Himalayan slopes searching for
pastures for their flocks of goats and sheep.

In Pahalgam, Gujar men looking to buy a horse check its age by
looking at its teeth.

On the banks of the Sindh River in the village of Wayil, a Bakkarwal
family is on the move to their home in the glaciers.

Gujar men heading for Chandanwari look for jobs helping the
pilgrims going to Amarnath carry their supplies.

Shoeing a horse in Pahalgam.

Glacier lake in Sheshnag.

Tourists on horseback in Sonamarg.

Sheep grazing in Sonamarg.

Man with his pony in Sheshnag.

A Gujar man crossing a makeshift bridge with his horse in Chandanwari.

A woman crossing the Lidder River in Pahalgam.

In the fall, farmers will buy bulrush reeds to make mats during the winter when they do not have any work to do. These mats are used as carpets in modest homes in Kashmir.

House engulfed by fog on an island in Dal Lake.

A foggy morning on Dal Lake.

Buying firewood on Dal Lake with the Hazratbal mosque in the background.

Flower vendor on his *shikara* in the early morning on Dal Lake.

A view of Lal Chowk in the old part of Srinagar.

A pundit's home (a Hindu home) that was abandoned at the height of
the unrest in the 1980s.

OVERLEAF: Tourists take an early evening ride in a *shikara* on Dal Lake.

175

An elderly couple on a *shikara* in the Hazratbal area.

A boat on Dal Lake near the Hazratbal area.

Boats on Dal Lake near Nehru Park area.

People shop in stores near Nehru Park area in early evening.

# Acknowledgments

First of all, I would like to thank Pascale Debord Slama for introducing me to Kashmir and suggesting that I make a book.

I would also like to express my gratitude to my editor Jim Mairs for believing and encouraging me in this project, and my gratitude as well to his assistant Austin O'Driscoll. Thanks to Laura Lindgren for her wonderful design. And thanks to Anne Day for introducing me to W. W. Norton.

Thanks also to my childhood friend Anil Thadani who was interested in photography before I was and then enthusiastically supported me in my work once I got started.

I am indebted to Olympus for their wonderful E-System cameras and lenses that helped me complete my project and for their Visionary Program that supports professional photographers.

Art Davidson and I would both like to thank Lassa, Bashir Butt, Ghulam Butt, Younis Anjum, and Usman Rahmad.

Technical Data:

Camera: Olympus E-1

Lenses: Olympus Zuiko 14–54mm, 50mm macro, 50–200mm, 90–250mm and 300mm.

A view of Dal Lake in the evening.

The Hazratbal Mosque in Srinagar is the most revered shrine of the
Kashmiris. Its history dates to the early seventeenth century.

A fisherman at dusk in his *shikara* with
the Hazratbal mosque in the background.

View from my houseboat in the morning on Dal Lake.

Rainbow over Dal Lake.

The Vale of Kashmir
John Isaac

Copyright © 2008 by John Isaac
Introduction copyright © 2008 Art Davidson

Book design and composition by Laura Lindgren
The text of this book is composed in Electra.

Manufactured by Mondadori Printing, Verona

Library of Congress Cataloging-in-Publication Data
Isaac, John.
    The Vale of Kashmir / John Isaac ; introduction by Art Davidson. — 1st ed.
        p.  cm.
    ISBN 978-0-393-06525-1 (hardcover)
    1.  Kashmir, Vale of (India)—Pictorial works. 2.  Kashmir, Vale of
(India)—Description and travel.  I. Title.
    DS485.K24I83 2008
    954'.6—dc22                                                          2008016852

W. W. Norton & Company
500 Fifth Avenue, New York, NY 10110
www.wwnorton.com

W. W. Norton & Company Ltd.
Castle House, 75/76 Wells Street, London, W1T 3QT

1 2 3 4 5 6 7 8 9 0